Bridgestone
BOOKS

Native American Life

The Northwest Indians

Daily Life in the 1700s

by Judy Monroe

Consultant:
Troy Rollen Johnson, PhD
American Indian Studies
California State University
Long Beach, California

Capstone
press

Mankato, Minnesota

Bridgestone Books are published by Capstone Press,
151 Good Counsel Drive, P.O. Box 669, Mankato, Minnesota 56002-0669.
www.capstonepress.com

Library of Congress Cataloging-in-Publication Data
Monroe, Judy.
   The Northwest Indians: daily life in the 1700s / by Judy Monroe.
   p. cm.—(Bridgestone books. Native American life)
   Summary: "A brief introduction to Native American tribes of the Northwest, including their social structure, homes, food, clothing, and traditions"—Provided by publisher.
   Includes bibliographical references and index.
   ISBN-13: 978-0-7368-4316-4 (hardcover)
   ISBN-10: 0-7368-4316-7 (hardcover)
   1. Indians of North America—Northwest Coast of North America—History—18th century—Juvenile literature. 2. Indians of North America—Northwest Coast of North America—Social life and customs—18th century—Juvenile literature. 3. Northwest Coast of North America—Antiquities—Juvenile literature. I. Title. II. Series.
E78.N78M65 2006
977.004'97—dc22   2005001653

Editorial Credits
Christine Peterson, editor; Jennifer Bergstrom, set designer; Ted Williams, book designer;
   Wanda Winch, photo researcher/photo editor; maps.com, map illustrator

Photo Credits
The Granger Collection, New York, 20
Illustration by Gordon Miller, cover, 8, 14, 18
Image courtesy of Bill Holm, 6, 10
McCormick Library of Special Collections, Northwestern University Library, 16
National Archives of Canada, C-33614/Canadian Heritage Gallery (ID#10048), 12

032010
5652VMI

Table of Contents

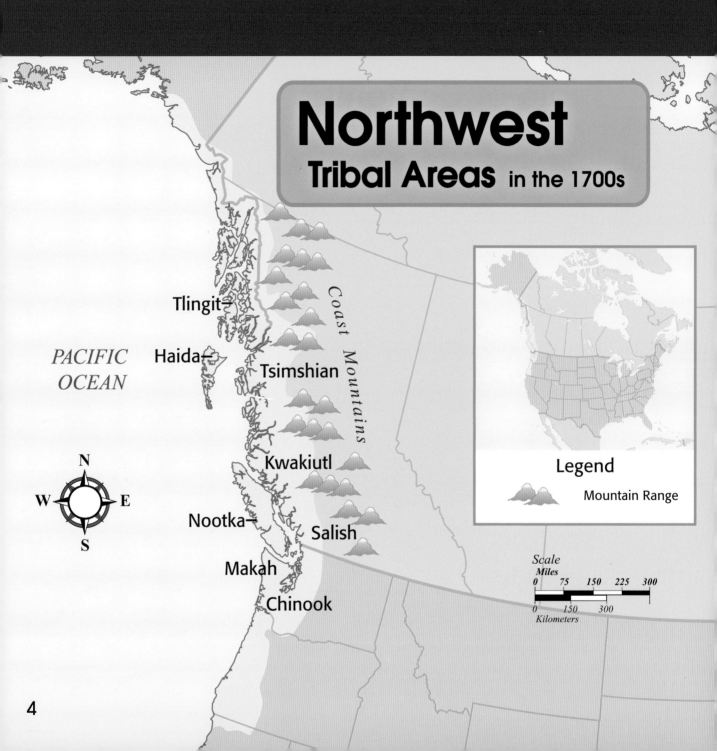

Northwest
Tribal Areas in the 1700s

PACIFIC
OCEAN

Tlingit

Haida

Tsimshian

Coast Mountains

Kwakiutl

Nootka

Salish

Makah

Chinook

N
W   E
S

Legend

Mountain Range

Scale
Miles
0   75   150   225   300

0   150   300
Kilometers

The Northwest and Its People

The waters and forests of the Northwest shaped the daily life of Native Americans. This area stretches from what is now northern California to Alaska. Native Americans have lived there for at least 10,000 years.

Until Russian explorers arrived in the late 1700s, Native Americans depended on the land for their needs. **Tribes** built homes from trees in nearby forests. They gathered food from the land and waters. For Northwest Indians, the forests and waters were part of their **thriving** culture.

◀ Historic tribal areas of Northwest Indians are shown over present-day borders of the United States and Canada.

Social Structure

In the Northwest, most Native Americans were part of large family groups called **moieties**. Most tribes had two moieties. Members of the Tlingit tribe belonged to either the Raven or Eagle moiety.

Families also formed smaller groups called **clans**. Clans followed a woman's side of the family. Most clans lived together in villages. Male chiefs ruled clans and villages.

Everyone in a village had jobs. Men and boys hunted and fished. Women and girls gathered plants for food and medicines.

◀ In the Northwest, chiefs often visited neighboring tribes to talk about trades.

Homes

Native Americans gathered wood from forests to make their homes. They searched the forests for cedar trees. This wood stayed strong in the wet **climate**. Men built large cedar homes called plank houses. They fit large wooden posts and boards together without nails.

Some people lived in large moiety houses near the ocean. These cedar houses had beds, benches, and fire pits. About 100 people lived in a single moiety house.

◀ Some Northwest tribes built their homes facing the ocean to honor nature.

Food

Northwest tribes got their food from the land or water. For most tribes, salmon was the main food. Men caught salmon with spears, nets, and traps. In the far north, men hunted whales in the ocean. Men also hunted animals in the forests.

In the summer, women gathered berries, roots, and bird eggs. They found snails and clams along the beach. Women dried extra food for winter.

◀ Makah men used long spears to hunt whales in the icy ocean waters off the Northwest coast.

Clothing

Women wove materials from nature into clothing. They wove tree bark, roots, and grasses into cloth. They made skirts, shirts, and pants. This cloth dried quickly when wet. People also wore hats shaped like cones to keep out the rain. In colder areas, women used animal skins to make soft shoes called moccasins.

Many people wore earrings and nose rings made of shell or bone. Women and girls wore lip or chin pegs made of bone or wood.

◄ Nootka Indians wore hats, shirts, and blankets made from cedar bark.

Trading and Economy

Northwest tribes traded for things the land and water did not provide. They traded goods that were special to their area. The Tlingit filled canoes with furs, blankets, and fish to trade. The Kwakiutl traded shells. Nootka Indians brought whale bones for tools and whale oil for light.

People often traveled great distances to trade goods. Tribes from the coast would carry baskets of goods across mountains to trade with inland tribes. Other groups traveled north to trade with Arctic tribes.

◄ Northwest tribes caught fish to trade with other tribes.

Leisure Time

Most Northwest tribes enjoyed playing guessing games. The hand game was popular in many tribes. One person hid a small bone in one hand. Other players tried to guess which hand held the bone. Children also played guessing games. They tossed sticks, bones, or colored stones. Players guessed how the objects would land.

Children also learned skills through play. Boys learned to use large canoes by using smaller ones. Girls cared for dolls made from wood and grass to learn child care.

◀ Haida Indians play the hand game in 1893. Rules for the game have not changed in hundreds of years.

Traditions

In the Northwest, tribes held **potlatches** to celebrate events. Clan leaders held these **ceremonies** for births, weddings, and other events. It took months to prepare the food and gifts for a potlatch.

A potlatch lasted several days. Hundreds of guests sang, danced, and told stories. The leader gave everyone gifts, such as baskets, blankets, or pots. These gifts were a sign of the chief's money and power.

◄ Tlingit dancers wore colorful costumes for potlatches.

Passing On Traditions

Native Americans told stories to pass on traditions. Northwest tribes told stories about how their land and people began.

The Tlingit told stories about a Thunderbird who lived on top of the highest mountain. The Thunderbird could start a storm by flapping its wings.

People also shared history through art. The Haida and other tribes carved **totem poles**. Animals and symbols on these poles told the history of a clan. Today, these poles remind Native Americans of their past.

◄ Northwest tribes carved totem poles to share their history with others. Many totem poles still stand today.

Glossary

ceremony (SER-uh-moh-nee)—formal actions, words, or music performed to mark an important occasion

clan (KLAN)—a large group of related families

climate (KLYE-mit)—the usual weather in a place

moiety (MOY-uh-tee)—one of two large family groups in a tribe

potlatch (POT-lach)—a special gathering that includes a feast and gift-giving

thrive (THRIVE)—to do well

totem pole (TOH-tuhm POHL)—a pole carved and painted with animals and other objects that represent a family

tribe (TRIBE)—a group of people who share the same language and way of life

Read More

Ansary, Mir Tamim. *Northwest Coast Indians.* Native Americans. Des Plaines, Ill.: Heinemann, 2000.

Kamma, Anne. *If You Lived With the Indians of the Northwest Coast.* New York: Scholastic, 2002.

Internet Sites

FactHound offers a safe, fun way to find Internet sites related to this book. All of the sites on FactHound have been researched by our staff.

Here's how:
1. Visit *www.facthound.com*
2. Type in this special code **0736843167** for age-appropriate sites. Or enter a search word related to this book for a more general search.
3. Click on the **Fetch It** button.

FactHound will fetch the best sites for you!

Index